The Dark Time of Angels

Also By Pier Giorgio Di Cicco

We Are the Light Turning 1975 *(Revised,* 1976*)*
The Sad Facts 1977
The Circular Dark 1977
Dancing in the House of Cards 1977
A Burning Patience 1978
Dolce-Amaro 1978
The Tough Romance 1979, 1990
translated as Les amours difficiles 1990
A Straw Hat for Everything 1981
Flying Deeper into the Century 1982
Dark to Light: Reasons for Humanness Poems 1976-1979 1983
Women We Never See Again 1984
Post-Sixties Nocturne 1985
Virgin Science: Hunting Holistic Paradigms 1986
Living in Paradise – New and Selected Poems 2001
The Honeymoon Wilderness 2002

As Editor

Roman Candles: An Anthology of Seventeen Italo-Canadian Poets 1978

Pier Giorgio
Di Cicco

The Dark Time of Angels

Mansfield Press

National Library of Canada Cataloguing in Publication

Di Cicco, Pier Giorgio, 1949-
The dark time of angels / Pier Giorgio Di Cicco.

Poems.
ISBN 1-894469-14-3

I. Title.

PS8557.I248D37 2003 C811'.54 C2003-905349-0

COVER DESIGN: *Gabriel Caira & Angela Gulia*
TEXT DESIGN: *Denis De Klerck*
TECHNICAL ADVISOR: *Tim Hanna*
COVER PHOTO: *Daniel Diaz Arrasco*
AUTHOR PHOTO: *Glen McGuire*

The publication of *The Dark Time of Angels* has been generously supported by The Canada Council for the Arts and The Ontario Arts Council

Mansfield Press Inc.
25 MANSFIELD AVENUE, TORONTO, ONTARIO, CANADA. M6J 2A9
Publisher: *Denis De Klerck*
www.mansfieldpress.net

The awake lion must prowl for God
in places it once feared.

–St. John of the Cross

Dedicated to Mario Romano

Table of Contents

Angel of Writing – 9
Gabriel – 11
Medias Res – 12
Construed – 14
Like a Frail Angel – 16
Attendance – 18
It is Not Love I Seek – 20
The Lone Prairie – 21
Desert Song – 22
The Garden Angel – 24
A Letter East – 25
My Mother's Son – 27
Palm Sunday – 28
Ad hominum – 30
Listening to a Boy's Confession – 32
O Rushing Fantasy – 34
The Visitor – 37
Praying – 39
Hell: a continuance – 41
Cusp – 43
Night Visiting Song – 45
Walking to the Fridge at Night – 47
Fighting Angels – 48
The Wilderness Is Yet The Garden – 51
Demons with Full Names – 52
Son – 66
Death Knocks – 68
Ramble – 70
Alive Again – 71
Confession – 73
How to give in to the world – 75
Changed – 77
Transmogrified – 78
Desert Song II – 80
God as Moths – 82
Surrounding Angels – 85
At the Colorado – 87
Supplanting – 89
Easter – 90
The Prayer – 92

Angel of Writing

angel of writing
look after me,
bring goodness where
you want it, chase badness
from the angels of malignancy,
rise from the grasses of even the
cold snows, the imperishable green
gladness of unexpectancy, rise
and do your bidding.

angels of goodness and
impenetrable longing,
heal the wounds of my forgotten.
bring what needs to be done and undone,
correct my every movement,
nudge me like a blind man nudged
gently across streets, places of
loved ones, lived in.

do not absolve of what is not
our business, but His.
be thou working,
straighten my fingers
to the stem of wavering plants,
give a little courage where I fear,
tread without wings, disturb
nothing with your flutter;
make me out to be less a man,
and a priest of a brother
who is willing to have a coffee
amidst the ranges and the towns
of helter skelter and blessing.

my writing angels, let us not have too
much pathos and too much laughter;
let us keep the hearth fire burning
just right; let not my
skin grow cold, arrange my brains
in a cartography that does the world
some good while it does
what it must
in illness and wonder.

angels behind everything seen, not
to be seen. do, beyond me and
despite me, reshape my
words, misbegotten by me;
sunshine of them where my heart
darkens, gift of evil, transform,
leave me to burn.
be they seeds or not, my words,
rise like the morning light,
inveterately with my handfuls,
my verbiage, and let it commence,

the day for someone.

Gabriel

gabriel in the dark,
blowing your horn
what do you say to me in
fanfare, dropped pencils, birds
arraigned on eaves, news of the dead,
your notes, how
I have heard you all my life
corralling the stars and things,
inaugurating cities, dreams,
installments of illusion. you would I
were deaf for all the mistaken;
tireless trumpeter, whom I wear on my
arm like a hawk, whom I blast in my head
like foreboding,
saving that great tune for last,
the gatherer of all contralto, my grief,
my bad conscience, my sublime.
you will weave them all into a meaning
that wakes God, and he will put his hand
on my head, and bid me sleep
out of my mournful life.

Medias Res

at the age of fifty you begin to
fend for yourself if you go crazy no
one will look after you
so you hole up
you make sure your grief is respectable to you.
you avoid small girls and small dogs.

you bury particular people
you avoid themes
it takes a long time not to panic and look
for mom or doc holliday,
the cavalry are all dead,
jesus like death takes on discernible features.

when you are fifty
God is extempore; he is in my valise,
my precious pain. the picnicker.
he picnics with me.
I forgot the jam. the ants carry me off.
they will make a house of me, a beautiful house
to house critters.

moon, blue moon,
river, lover, look at me.

songs from the fifties –
slow tunes that remind you of
a little boy scampering from
one milky way to another.
you would catch him like crazy.

you write faster and faster
anything will do
to brighten your day.

hope is assailing throngs of youth
on street corners.
you are not sure
if it's vanity or ignorance.
hope looks like many
things until it's naked; then it looks like
a soul, and you don't wonder
why it didn't get fed, given the state of the world
and the scraps people are happy with.

there are no golems, there are no maidens.
I am maw, ravenous man, made to make do
with birch and ravine;

the angel of madness I am.

Construed

from here the lights of the highway
are distant as the purpose of the world.
God sends flies and the usual, mortgage rates,
happiness, an extra twenty years we won't know what
to do with.
keeping still in the meditation of the cactus perplexes him.
I do not think he even wonders.
a man searching for meaning is his least
favourite thing, is my guess.
it is what we do – this meaning thing;
he's just a boy in summer with feet
draped in a pool; he barely hears what's
called to him from over his shoulder, from the house.
there was, in fact, something vain about
mother shouting for us to come in,
for whatever seemed important.
we had it right not wanting to come in from
the temple of sassafras and worm.

now that I remember we monks did little more than
that; we polished floors, made beds at the
instruction of superiors, but left to our own, we'd fish,
or muse about flies, as if their
movements told the errant wisdom of God;
we thought nothing of killing flies; because
to God one thing was not more important than
another, and the point was to walk to Him
resignedly. it didn't mean we couldn't laugh,
but we swatted the flies down the way
he painted a sunset or left a hole
for you to sprain your foot in. something about nonchalance –
not indifference to what hurts.

the meaning of God is just another room,
a field, a space to occupy, and laughter as you swat
a fly and miss.

if brother ninian read this, he'd nod and say
let's go fishing; he'd smile to say
I'd done something with good will,
and not understandably important.
there was always one more room,
another afternoon, and the putting of your head to the
pillow. we had no mothers,
though they came to the gates, to visit,
but we could not hear them
above the rush of leaves.
God sent them like flies, the annoying and concerned
voices, with God giving lessons as we splashed our feet,
while he spoke of grass and stars,
of sun and bees, and the confluence felt
like a doing of nothing; a placement of everything, now that
I think of it, is what He taught, and the rush
to understand was like the noise of trucks and things.

as I look at the distant highway, I feel like a
boy in a man's clothes I have grown into too quickly...
I feel like the wide eyes of the world waiting for
innocence; or maybe just like an orphan, so used
to being alone, that tears are something I do not have,
but that others have for me;
and that so much meaning, as the world has, I do not miss.

Like a Frail Angel

like a frail angel in the sight of God
I came, strumming my ribs, through
overblown landscapes, accessing
my baby's heart. my doyenne eyes;

accessing these woods and that, any old
ghost walking into
this dumb, found creation, setting up
pansies, any old sureness kicked aside and
waiting.

✧

close to the
poem I came, bowed,
genuflected in my bones,
doubled over brain, paid my respects.

✧

became his siphoning, His mouth, His
lungs, stuttered one; in one belch,
a world. and cataracts and trees like melodies.
His exact intent, moons and eyes, song archives;
created for this, legato, for His make,
I sat imperial for the moments take;
lest child and flower missed the chreode
of his wonderment, I vigil stood,
enthroned in Him, iconoclasting, betting and
blessing whim and joyous foundling. while his serene
smile glutted the clouds.
once, more, I involuted the kicks, and
desirous of Him, wished a lining for the world
I could be of, like skin. so
beautiful.
His vision.
a wet blanket, a sun going down,
my attempt, a failure visioning.

✧

like a frail angel in the sight of him,
I shuck his wants and find intent,
emissary of the thing and else for Him.

Attendance

you take so much.
you take everything.

I have nothing.
it is all gone. look not even a story.

how remarkable.
look how the loon, the wild dog and the willow
remain,
to be seen, to be heard,
hankering for my emptiness.

so much love, your emptying.

no story, do you want a story?
it is written on my brow.
my features. you write.
they will know of your letters.

here is one called song,
bent, like my stoop.

you could have upturned it like a
question mark.
what are you going to do for song now
that I listen to everything?

new music.
I am cooking a sausage at 5 in the morning,
waiting for new music. the stars
come in, they
mix with dawn.

perhaps it is not new music at all.
you want it all to keep quiet, this

brash hoping,
this beauty shoved aside; the fear of you along-
side the love of you, the kiss
of cold creation.

It is Not Love I Seek

It is not love I seek
It is the wood and assorted
Ghosts of God, my friends and
Diatribes of darkness; it is not
Angels I beseech although
I sought them out for signs
Under a carapace of wonder.
It is my mortality, strung
On the finest breath,
It is the bird at dawn, it's first
Grey note piercing history, making the
Most of chance, as if a trumpeter,
But just one more lame thing
Crowning glory.
It is not love I seek, for I do love,
Everywhere, I lay my life to the pillow.
I have not failed to love.
I failed to hate the dark and so,
I am naked of air, an image to be replete,
I am cross unsleeved of flesh,
I am transfiguration,
That nexus where sacrament and
Brain-hollow meet; my life unfilled, poured like
Niagara, caught in the turbines,
Where so little of me is made
To light the one grey note of thrush –
An understanding of so little that I am.

The Lone Prairie

I will not write today, what
with my mother's photograph and the dead ones
looking at me, as if I were the last survivor – I tell
their stories, with a vengeance, with an appetite for what
ate them. I eat the stars and moons for them. I finish off their
meals; death walked in, God walked in with
his dull waiter – I was allowed to go on, to spit at destiny, to be
hauled by the teeth by God, to inscribe these stones with
bare hands,
hands that held doves, that caressed a baby's cheek,
hands raised in supplication, hands made for
scratching the heart onto wood, and metal and air, and in
your mind trying so hard to make a monument of life –
some statue that would console the human creature.

I will not write today. I am allowed to go on,
and do the inexorable, walk like a mouth into the raw sun –
and speak the dead,
enduring of devils and saints – like a last continent,
I offer my hand to God, and ask him why, wrenching him into
the human condition. I account for him,
and bring him down, this perfector, for whom tears
are just brine, to eat at words and eat at them and eat at them,
until there is only me –
the mirror he wants for himself,
poor, blind benevolent one, poor God.

Desert Song

I basically don't want to be with anybody,
but you, wise saw, who leaves me in the wilderness
with the wind banging on the door, with every year
trying to get in to wake me out of my sheepish self
into the murder of my heart. for my heart must be murdered,
it has done no good hungering and bleating. it wanted to be
water, but I could not swim, oh so much I have resisted,
especially the desert; for all its palms and cactus, it was the
horned toad who wanted to be my friend, the speckled
rattler, the coyote coming up to me in the dark – it was myself
gnashing in the dark that I needed to befriend –
it was my isolate boyhood, tearing its skin off to find
evil just a horror of myself and goodness just a part of me –
my hungers and fears were my own, every poem
a way to say so, slowly, ever slowly; in the twilight of
my time, I am ready to mulch clouds and be
my own.

I see Christ no differently than this, but
with strangely localized brown eyes from a part of the world – I
am through with divinity being anywhere else –
the transcendent is what you stop and gawk at
when your fingers have brushed the
strings of creation
and you hear god in thistles and bramble-weeds.

I am ready to be in the wilderness I have lived in,
without consolation.

I was saying mass at the chapel,
and my view is straight outside the door
and, like a dervish, a dust storm
appeared; the children of God quaked in their seats, but
I had no notion but to be welcoming of death or accident or
provident ending hands; I said, it is my
cause not to be afraid,
and I am through seeking for shelter from the call,

be it His madness, or anger or respite – whatever
death is called, let it be like a lonesome animal come
to feed, let it be the hound of His mercy –
let my stupidity be barren and naked beneath His wandering
sight.

and whoever these words are for, let them be as
tendrils of my vulnerability, exposed to chance and
His goodness; let me be punished, as will, and blighted
with coronations on my eyes.
what I merit, is beyond me,
may what I have given, as reward, embrace me
as a newborn babe, held up to the elements –
where never dark, His grace.

The Garden Angel

there is the angel that looks after me.
there in the garden,
poking his head up between the
weeds;
he is the one that looks after me, I think,
although I brought him, stole him away from
the christmas manger,
'cause I needed him more than baby jesus
or the wise men, who'd already found
salvation and a glorious show.
through snow and dew and rain that
angel's stood there. for a while, he was pinned
to the wall of the shed, and the wind nudged
him left and right, mainly to the right.
he shows up in photographs
and memories. what exactly he did
for his keep is beyond me.
clearly he was only a namesake for the
powers that watched me sleep and kept
my anger from frothing and nudged me
away from the fear of the barn and falling trees.
what he did was watch me, and busied himself
in ways I did not know.

angel I bow before you, away from
wind-chimes
and cupidons;

there you are in the weeds,
as if your wings were still, like any
thing propped against the fence.
such power,

in the garden,
as if it were not paradise inverted,
laughing under stars as if each one were
not a prayer for the awakened love.

A Letter East

when I arrived here
I was naked, loved only by wood
and brush, and was clothed gradually,
by the night and stars;
sounds would come over the fields and
I would shape them to familiar things.
I had brought a crucifix and would look
at it only askance and vaguely,
for fear I would become less corporeal
than I was... after a long time, my poverty
looked like a man hanging; it is as if he were hardly on the cross
but would walk with me, my voice becoming his,
or was it his voice becoming mine; hardly, because I realized
after a while it was
like the sea, washing the same detritus back to me,
but transformed, corralled, sometimes shining,
to make me think what I had thrown away
was worth... what?... something about tears and anger
becoming tough skin, or self-hurt becoming a hair of compassion.
something about artifice being his, and me the clay, – or if that's
predictable, something about treating the animals more gently,

but let it go.
I am still naked, by all definitions,
and the night sky does not seem cold,
though it is well into october; some snow has arrived
on the mountain ash berries and the still surviving leaves;
I sense something of me in that. it is beautiful, the snow-capped
green and red, and I am still man enough not to see the beauty of
it in myself – of how contrasts make for the lovely, hurt as they do.

I admit however of not being afraid of bandits or thieves.
I welcome them; no matter what the month brings.
there is that much providence in the branches and stars,
and not the kind of providence that makes things better for a while,
but the kind that knows you will come home no matter what.

in the springtime, I shall write again. I shall have new metaphors,
and they will mean something different.
what I will have learned is waiting somewhere along the brushline
in the cleft where the pines are.

maybe it will be like a good dog, that shadow I now am a little
leery of. there is nothing in the world that you must send
right now, for all the love you owe me or have given me.

My Mother's Son

he's the heavy package.
unyou, the dead brother, stillborn
of me, I carry. he took
the colour from the rose – what
I use to beat myself. he's the image
that comes to mind.

a dead infant
between me and everyone.
this shame, this uninviting
to the world.
he is a world war,
or the spawn of grief.

when they cut the umbilicus they
cut nothing. he got through.
the corpuscles,
the names of trains, whatever.

there are two in me, talking.
neither a good angel nor a bad one.
it weighs.
I am not Christ to it,
I redeem him
by carrying him to term.

it is stuff that wraps my
bones like a worm,
a coupled thing.

I do not welcome it,
forgive or kill.

I sit and stare at my fingers working out
mortality

to see which of us will come to
an ending.

Palm Sunday

out of the hell of self comes my Lord,
bodied, filling my bones, brandishing losses
and calling my lies, leaving them around
me like sticks and bits, my Lord
comes, escorted by no angels
and apparitions himself on the mood
of my grief and hope.

on this palm sunday, He empties me
of death and deadens me, among the bright
arms of spring and bark so desiccated,
dry, He lets my arms be arms of a cross
with blood murmuring what must be of me,
a shell, a tatter;
He must be forever what I do not want,
the metaphysic of a man crying,
becoming what must seem to me
a loss of world,
loved.

I wish He had two angels to escort Him
or anything pretty, and decorating
senses, and the crop that is the field,
and intertwining branches that look like
friends walking arm in arm,
instead of this breath expiring like
an emptied cup, this barren,
this thirst that will not drink
what only can restore,
my love for everything,
unnamed of me.

my eyes hurt from the plain sun,
because I will not look
up with my soul.
I will not be transformed
but I will write to Him, of Him,

as He dredges my arms to
the sorrowful, to take on
suffering, until I feel,
expert in nothing, not joy,
just desire to alleviate,
and suck the wound of venom from
my sister, world, and plant a kiss
like dawn
that will not wake her.

I am distressed in Him, this sunday
of a passion yet to come.
desirous of Him, like my pity turned on
Him. bedfellow I would nurture

or like a flower in the heap,
I would reach in and gripping my own heart
offer Him sacrifice,
so I would sleep a dream
of simple man,
unchanged, brought nowhere;
what I cannot be, like the dead
kissed back to life, must resurrected
stand and close my eyes,
as simply as a leafy branch
blessing the cold may lilies.

Ad Hominum

you want me to talk about
my faith and I come out sounding like
the catacombs. alright;

I collect things,
like blood and tears.

I live where wine
becomes blood and bread, flesh.

it's fantastic, not as preposterous
as having an idea of who I am.
I was spared that
when I learned to beg;

so many voices
without interpretations.

we all drink with one tongue
warbling the
foul note of need.

reduced to
thirst,

like a soul scratching to be let in.

to live or die;
that's about it.

and I have dreams in which
I find you,
your weak heart shouting
love me for who I am;
and that sounds fair enough,
like a balloon of words above your slender
and forsaken arms
my wife, my lovely world,
you.

Listening to a Boy's Confession

are
you listening, he asks.

you might say so,
and he makes me chuckle;
I have been listening like a heart
in my hand
for a millennium
at least I think a heart in the hand
listens,
like my guts then, embedded in a rising
star,
or a man so eager to swathe his brother
in bones that are healed.
I have been listening like the oracular turned
inward, listening for oceans
and the return call to the saviour.

he has not been to confession for five years
and he has been calling out for a sparrow
unfearful of the branch he is, creation
visiting him like grace, and I have been listening
for him where I hardly know I am,
in hope for a world resurrecting,

and if I look as if I have been falling asleep
it is the burden of so many
failed kisses and lies on my back,
the lies to get to an open field and let the sun
make flesh of a scarecrow heart,
the impoverished human crying
for exoneration, citizenship,
innocence.   I listen alright;

I have done nothing but. he is stunned,
my boy in the sacrament, when I say yes and chuckle
he has this gaze that says *where do I go next,*

and *what are my sins... are they important,*
do you hear them, priest? they have been
travelling companions for so long I want direction
where they might be laid like a sack by the road...
he wants this from me and I realize his consternation at my
chuckle bewilders him, though deep inside he's heartened
by anything, something, not taking his burden as seriously
as love, for him, the love the cosmos has behind
shrubs and leaves, waiting to soothe his boyish brow.

I am remembering him a loving universe,
remember it for myself;
and I laugh also I know for my own ludicrousness,
for the boy I am layered with bones,
puffed up and tired
from a world of disbelief...

and I remember my chuckle in the stars
and wanton absolutions on the summer nights
when I was young,
and nothing took my sin so seriously
as myself, loving me as the sky did
and the air between the choked screams
of adults, and most any little thing I looked at...
there was that chuckle, as I told the unforgivable
tale of myself to the planet,
there was a sash around my head that God
changed, just to give me a different colour,
just to play with me, just to remind me
that the world's grief was an opportunity
to fall into his grace,
so wanton,
unknotted of fear,
where only crucifixion was made
of forgetting it.

O Rushing Fantasy

Tonight I have swallowed my own
by the angel's bidding.
I prayed and I got what
I wanted; His truth, accomplished
by my own lies.
He has brought me around to the
place at the stream
from which to drink either poison
or water; depending on which day
I have cast the dice of my self in the
air, depending on which greed
gnarls my hand, depending on
which illusion I can not do
without, that day.
But tonight I have swallowed my own.
My needs lie like pups on the floor;
my ruinations of others
waltz merrily past the kitchen
and go out and hang themselves,
calling my name.
The angels don't laugh, although they
might, were they a lot like me.
I have brought myself to drink
the foul thing that I am,
and it has refreshed me
in the dark place I had no mind to
go to; in my gut that was so careful
about tidbits,
I have found the truth with a
vague call from childhood,
like a horizon with a lonely tree.
And the truth spells omnipotence,
a cry, a wastage and a purge –
nothing I ever liked.
To do things not for myself;
that is another malicious thing done
to me of His mercy,

and to forego what I needed
that I might have a special
canyon beaten from my middle
so His waters can flow.
Self-emptying, they call it, done
by grazing your head
against the spikes of event
and history; look, without an
aesthetic to rosy you, you meet
the blank incarnation of His eyes
where you see only yourself;
and it is the beginning,
whether you look poor and ragged,
beseeching in your eyes,
or just evil;
and then you ask for more; either
way it is a start. But first you swallow
your own;
what you have done to satisfy yourself,
backing up, like the gorge
of world, frantic and in love
without; you swallow what you merit
like yourself,
and you see the insufficiency,
rotten nakedness.

Oh what will it take to make me
serviceable, this awful drinking,
this immolation that I do myself
rather than lie down and let Him waft me
like the dandelions blown from yellow,
like the earth made green for no one
but the rain.
What will it take to understand
the angels keep quiet just to
refrain from your eyes
a power that would crush
or coddle like a mother.
What I drink tonight be of use.
Some understanding like a path

be readied. For though I may not
walk out of the judgement I have
seen in myself, may others walk in
and find a garden, or a leaf –
that memorial, my sin.
Simply, what must be crushed,
made new creation – as simple a thing
as a leaf; that distillation of what I drink
so foul, exchanged for anything
of worth.

The Visitor

when the angel came, we were in various places;
he came at five when I was in bed, he came at 5 in the
afternoon for someone – they stagger the hours – angels do –
to make it seem like there's more than one,
or perhaps not to be seen, or just to enchant
with numerology – and the angel brought to one
forgiveness and blue light; and made the day seem sunny
in a cave of grief; for another, the angel healed
the bones and filled the room like a godmother; to another
he brought understanding of the kind that can sever
the hold we make on each other.
it was the angel of release – unmistakable, we all felt it,
like a tremor from under the earth – some took it in stride,
like God's grace, others ran for shelter, others took it to mean
they had sorted things out one more time with wits and
strength.

I am practiced at angels. I know their coming, I see their
dog-eared remains of rooms and atmospheres;
I knew what he wanted – surrender and reprieve,
for the tired children of His gaze.
I marvelled again at how the drama stops at His behest.
I saw our will bent to His mercy, and how the angel was
like a forearm to Him.
whenever an angel leaves I see the rooms so empty, before I
fill them again with need and fear. I see the air
unfabricked of them, and marvel there is so much room
in the world without their wings, of which they have none;
they do not stand out – this kind;
their knowledge is of you and of your eyes,
and you would see as they do,
what must be done, forgiving of what has been done.

✧

oh sublime fathering sense,
how I have yearned to spell you out and only incurred
your intervention.
let me say it was only my hurt and greed
that lived here.
I would add a few things – to be taken back to heaven before
they disappear – your angels... but they do what they came to do
and have done with it; there is beyond the sentence of Your will
no addition and heart-felt scrubbing.
but there is so much I would have added to the angel's leaving
– how not to do this and that,
questions that would have made me wise before I'm old,
lessons on how to kiss as gently as the wind that blows puff-balls
from the tops of thistles.

there is one more thing I wish to know, always,
before I resume my patience
for your rain. there is one grand thing
I need to know, and am pushed to it, like hunger,
and the question almost escapes me in the dull
wake of your angel; it has to do with how I should
look like Your mercy upon myself and how to wind
my fingers around
another's hand with the self-same touch – how to whisper
softness through the tendrils of my earthly frame,
and not bother a hair on anyone; not bother the baby's cry,
nor the lover's dream; how not to bother any small thing, as You
do...
and still be a man, with so much want.

Praying

you shut up. you listen,
you speak, you go about your daily chores.
you carry an alarm clock in your
pocket that explodes stars when
he says so... you grow an extra set of ears,
you walk with your antennae under the ground,
you listen with your heart beat,
and pain. you take news of hope from the
other side of the planet, like the leaves
around you, not so seriously...
he sings. he doesn't.
you get used to answers in the alphabet
of dust and death, and the baby's cry
pierces like a lozenge in your middle,
melting in the stars.

you dance and don't. you prepare yourself
with illusion or without, by giving away what you
love best, or holding on to what's loved most.
he is not fussy, for your cranium, to have you
deafened still.
he will have you any old way
so that it looks like grace.

and now you sing the song of your guts,
wanting out. you sing the sublime,
and the little darlings that he gave you,
so you think, and he will not
measure you by your thankfulness,
but by your surprise at the awful
maw of night he is, breaking into bright
horizon.

there are many ways to be with him and so few
to be with yourself.
here you are propped against a planet
by apparent need, and circumspect fear
and he will have the grass whisked from under
your feet until his palm is all you stand on, looking
goofy and oh-so-full of what rakes you, hungered
of yourself – His glory, smashed like a lover's kiss
inside your thick and lowing brain – the hot
kamikaze of your love.

HELL: A CONTINUANCE

I hear laughter, in my bones.
or is it love.
it should be shameful.

it is pretty much the same,

the death of comedy.

jack has had his jill.
the sins of omission
piled outside the door.
the robin is hoarse.

I get no more letters from the dead.
the reasons, storks.

it is a cold winter.
bodies hang from the trees.

drunk with my hell,
reeling, carrying on with
wished for things,
named. chronicled like eyes
in different years.

do me. have done with me,
make me, finish me,
my worldly wants, my very
couldn't-be-done wants,
sun-cups, a hair or two on the saint
of a little boy you might have left alone,
to himself, to vagrant flowers.

my mother used to call me "gioia"
– joy... as I take that ride now
with lumps in my throat, I stutter
life-ward.
happy the man who knows such primal
tap-roots of himself and lies face down to
the grave, cursing dirt.

✧

I have been left to stew,
in the derelict, my sin.
what I have made of beauty,
and good will.
what the body does, decrepitude,
is nothing to my soul.

I could warn you.
it is done so easily, this damned thing.
bitterness, accrued; drops of blood
eroding, as a friend said, like stone... the
brain or heart like stone, like metaphor.

✧

to know what hell is
he gives me hell,
won't talk about it, no.
steeps me, paints in canvases,
blue birds, skies.
keeps me at it. whispered heaven.
break out break out, each bone cries.
not yet articulate, not yet eloquent
with mouth busted with spring cramming.
a statue of a man, proclaimed.
with bric-a-brac and doodads, life
around like pigeons, halo scorched to his
head, shouting with stone mouth, to
passersby and children.

Cusp

God of torture,
god of hell, god of mercy,
god of knell,

fix my bones up,
light my brain so I can walk
through the caverns of it,
not shouting.

god of anger and love,
god of the marmoset
and big arthritic bone,
god of juveniles and buttercup,

light my skin so that it
lights my bone, down the middle
where I can see my life walk,
seep,
down to the tendrils of my fingers
that would clasp hair like the
constellations,
that would tear wind down from
the snowy branch,

that would find rest, like the nest
my eyes are.

god of hunger and forsaken things,
know me as your
stalker; behind each unflowered thing
I watch your grace just miss,
or seconds late, blossom,
impossibly.

god of touch and robbery,
walk into my nakedness like a room.
all songs are our songs.

I am ready to lie alongside my mother,
gravewards and dance our fables into
moths, and drown our sins in an
iris called world,

and thread your will together
into what is meant, like a dream
we are the shadows of.

and I will baste you with my tears
in the knot of my passion,
until I am lowly, and you succumb to the beauty

of the stars and flowers you made so
glibly, in a fancy where you concocted me –
simple, impressionable man,
suckling creation.

Night Visiting Song

I don't know you.
I blew the "imminent" thing; just how
transcendent you are doesn't occur
to me until you send me lunacy,
send everyone away,
leave me with beavers and starlight.

I don't know you today.
you told me to love this thing and
that and they are waving goodbye
with their tiny hands,
hands that excavated me when they were
closer up.

I am weeping a big tear but it is more
like a metaphysical tear, very abstract
because I am dry as bone.

today you must paint yourself in the
air, today you must spell things out simply for me,
because I am grown stupid with second-guessing.
today you must come as a child in my arms,
though I have none,
as a lyric in a song,
today you must come
as grass, breeze, memory.

today I will look through the branches
propped against the sunset
and look for you peering
through the leaves changing your
face even as I speak it.

today linger.
stay awhile, for night is another
almanac I am not practiced at.

if you are to leave poetry
leave it on the doorstep where I will
pick it up when I am done with my meditation,
for it is you, not beauty, I thirst for,
and I am done mistaking you with your gifts.

today I do not know you,
but if you enter, I will be open minded with
my skull dredging up the derelict heart;
I will lift my spirits like a

man dressed for
starlight,

and I will sing the song of myself, visited.

Walking to the Fridge at Night

I am dying.
in a house.
in the country,
with rain that shouldn't be there.

a november that reminds me
of full novembers. a parade of loved
ones, dead or wounded, in the rain.

I am dying. it is a shout to them.
almost a yearning, the last note
on a sinking ship. it will get wet and
lost in oceanic dark. but here's the note.

I love my mother.
my sins have all been forgiven by someone
I don't know.
I walked the rain sometimes myself.

happy as a birthday party, my shout.
I could reach through the goddamn window
and touch you, late bloomers of my life,
whom now I love, now that I am naked

and shivering, excited by no less illusion
than what I entered with.

Fighting Angels

The angel must never be fought.
He comes to do what he will,
generally to smarten you up, aside from
all auspiciousness when you were asleep and loved;
but he must never be fought. when he turns
on you and says the stern –
you listen and don't revise
what he has told you of, you don't revise
His will, or you grow evil by defying His
grace. You don't,
when he has set you free, try on the shackles
of your need again. You don't presume
your sentimentality. You don't take
comfort in the familiar stroke.
You don't do anything. You shut up
and stomach the Father.
You learn obedience. He will not brook
your flair and argument. You do not
get what you want, finally.
You cannot choose to be freed, as He frees you.
Your destiny is to be saved from yourself.

They go away, the angels.
This is how they fight you. They go away
and leave the air blank;
there is a decided lack of meaning
in your life. You notice the air
stinks.
You notice you had guidance,
and now you don't. They fight you like this,
like you relied on them. How can you fight this
enemy that was your household, wife, and sister?

When you put your sword down,
you pray the omens become kisses;
you pray the woodwork becomes benevolent,
enchanted, you pray the mirror does not show you

what you are, hungry, loathful
with need and stridulent desire.
You pray for this – to look normal to yourself,
like a roadside flower, or any such thing.

And you promise not to fight again.
It is humility like a choke-hold from the inside.
You wince; your facial muscles are the choke-hold
on you that shows you kick grace like
a child that won't come out.
You are scared of flies and tick,
because your bitterness
is a boy in the dark, in the bramble,
in the wood.

They are not just porcelain and bronze,
garden cupidons and valentines.
They are the messengers and shadows,
they are revealers and powers.
They send flies and clap the air with accident,
like doors closing and dimensions.
They let you destroy yourself
and place your ecstasy. They can be good or bad
depending on whether your back breaks or bends
like a stalk in the wind.
Your damned will is what they salivate about,
your genuflection to love is what
melts them, makes them wet like a young girl
in the swoon of spring.
And you will learn to love and know what love is,
in the cold skin of understanding –
the new cold skin from which your body slithers,
the cold new skin that will be sky one day,
and soar like your eyes that now are wedded
to your tears.

You will fight them, and fall back into the
re-made man, ready to love anything outside
yourself.

But you must not fight them. It is beyond the
mercy of God – to design yourself, risking
that your lust for Him is great as He.
For if it is, you battle for eternity,
and you do not know if you are made of soft
or anger. You do not know what you are made of.
And thus it should be. As the dawn comes up
over the wilderness, take it as one more thing to know,
as a gift.

The Wilderness is Yet the Garden

how terrible to lose one's home
and yet, the heart, more terrible.

it is the era of invincible loss.

the wilderness is yet the garden
you must see through.

it is the dark to be vanquished.
it is the lone man, standing between himself
and thistle-rod.

it is the dogs of chance, more terrible,
you must befriend.

it is the boy in the field.
you must call to him. it is perhaps you; you
must guide him home by the sound, simply,
of your voice.

perhaps he knows of heaven, perhaps he doesn't.
perhaps you must tell him stories of it.
perhaps he will sing you to sleep.
who saves who?

you must be ready for the orphan you were.
and the orphan you are must take comfort for both of you.

you will see. you will have the strength between you to
mother each other, out of so much gentleness
from having run in the world, cold.

perhaps starlight will be in your handhold,
perhaps God,
and the wilderness will whisper nakedness, that will
not mean so much, when you are joined to yourself.

Demons with Full Names

The Song of the Hermit

this is the summer of death
of fireflies and burnt wood
where the orchestration of my life,
where the sieve breaks,
under barkwood and otter-screech,
where cars mosey into the headlight dark,
where my head hurts from wanting mamma
where my heart pitter-patters out of my ears;

... is a song of you,
mother of dreadful night,
mother who would not come to my aid,
your little orphan boy is scowling,
running in the prato, up the sleeve
of night.

I am not afraid of myself, of a few little words.
I wrap myself around the dead of summer.
I wake up mad, and my bones have gravity.
I speak like the long lost, and weave garlands for
children,
and I sleep with my demons.
I even drink cherry coke
and write letters to the dead,
who are not dead.
living is a vague ruse,
the eternal is now, the grave is my mouth,
that admits no one.
at last.

Demons

here is the demon,
bright as anything,
two faced;
he looks like your grandmother,
a cheque, a fresh installment.

I am a man of epic feelings.
so I tow the demon tightly,
he is happy to see me, but he knows
my throttle.

oh little one of so many words,
how do you dare to laugh at me,
when I, with a little laugh, could
snuff you out.

bombastic ones, out in the wood,
imitating coyotes and boyhood
faces gnarled with distress,
I shoot you in the eyes.

cupboard noises, dropped hatchets,
lattices creaking... you will lose your
voice, nattering like that
at me.

how many demons you are,
and sometimes one. I do not know you,
and I keep you like that, at a distance,
muttering among yourselves how to be
taken seriously.

what can I be afraid of,
after you shouted from my mother's coffin,
when you turned over like a loved one
after I said "amen".

when I have seen your own face
in my mirror, what do you hope for?
you of little sprite, my vanity.
I sing you to sleep, like a mother,
that you may go out and scare anew,
tomorrow.

look what you've done to my bony fingers
and my sanguine eyes, these years
of bad betrothal.

I marry you to my grave
and live.

The Demon Speaks...

I love you, like grass, like hair.
Be with me. Look in the mirror. Do not be
afraid of what you see when you see me.
I am naked and you must clothe me.

The Angel...

I have been out in the cold for so long
with my bright wings waiting.
I have come as a moth, a badger, a ray of light.
You have not seen me when you needed me.
I am the air around you. I fill all the air
with what you are blind to, what embraces you.

your will must strike the air
and burn to jasmine.

The One Called Despair.

god knows how he got in.
through the back door.
the window's open.

the spirit's broken.
he knew it.
hangs out behind every tree,
crying crash into me.

maybe my mother's there
with some old johnny mathis songs
and I just don't hear right.

says death
says waste
says the foregone.

Demons II.

this one comes from the left.
this one from the right.

not so dumb as to appear
as illusion. as the real. that one's
good.

here comes one as a scared rabbit,
the habitual,
what I do over and over again,
as if I were a coin.

here's one who says who I am,
the love of obstinacy,
the doo-doo I was born as.

the one as immolation, looking like
the love of God,
like underwear inside out.

and I tear and weep;

argh! wrestling loose,
my compadres, my happy
teamwork... I will use you as incisors
to mulch clouds.

you gather like washerwomen.
let us talk.

which one of you will escape
with who I am?

✧

and the demon meets the angel;
there is the brush of wings

and a doused sound.
there is nothing of the sort.
it is me again, shutting the door

✧

the demons come
with full names

Cornelius had them in
his cell, he hissed at them.
they hissed back.

they are not lust and anger,
they are deprecatory,
make you worthless shit,
come in sound and flurry.

and say go mad
you are alone.

I am alone,
no one loves as well as me.
home is something I can't spell, write
anymore.
my mother is buried five million miles away,
my skin is fading into bark and starlight...

the mad one was the newest
face, who made my face look rank by
morning light.

✧

                    the one that said you like
me, you live with me,

you've known me all your life,
no one can do the housework as well,
no one has come between us,

you love me as yourself, not at all...
we are beautiful, perfect, one.

write me a poem. so I did,
this gender free goody,
he said be for me like you were to God.
be with me for a while. all songs are the same.
it is the singing you want.

the angels made me drop things to
remember. they showed their faces on
cards and walls, sent a song about love,
and I grimaced (as close a thing as
genuflection)

and said God will not leave me.

The Demon of Kill Yourself.

he says
do not read hope,
find the tree and crash into it.

why not. the whynot bird.
you have been working so hard on your life.
give it up.

I have drawn your face
according to sick
and blame.
I have drawn your mother of oaf
and earth

I am dowager of loss and spite,
your very own hubby.

come into the circle where we sing
and remember nothing of
your valentines.

✧

darnel, hemlock, fever.
the words that sew together, you'll
never get.

house, garden, gate.
how do you solstice love?

✧

chorus

there are so many of us
we slice ourselves in two and threes
for you.
there is never enough of us
we want to fill the world for you
until there is only your heart
with a hatch,
out which we want to see you fly home.
home, home,

The Demon of Down

come in my little fellow,
come into the dark where you will
see yourself, unrecognizable or not

we have a picture for you, a room
all your aunties are waiting

swing from your chandelier tears
dance on your knuckle
come into the dark

and be afraid of nothing
for you have seen everything

what can scare you
certainly not us
we are the crickets of day
by night

we are the blind cat with
no luck

come into the brush
and be yourself

oh brave little one,
enfolded.

The One Named Alone

who dropped me here at three
years of age
who sang me to sleep never

who danced with me at my
brother's funeral
who I met in every bar from here to
bowling green.

hat's off, toodle-oo, I'll see you
at grave's end,
for whom I kill myself to come home.

how have things been? are the
wife and children okay?

singing between oceans
swinging a tiny harmonica
waving my sister like a laurel
my cameo of mother
my head for a locket.

coming for an afternoon visit.
the two of us, in big empty chairs,
discussing wind,
strategies, nerves.

what can I offer you.
did you have my arms, delusions?
is the air cold?
who is shivering in the abyss?

my name without a voice.

you cannot move,
he blathers, you cannot
out of vicious circle love, hope;
death, life, rest,
like electrical things,
thwarted like electrons, like
sparkles doused.

sleep in the burn of body,
let light weigh you down,
let chore look wall-like,
let paralysis, like ancient boyhood ogre
gnash at the foot of the bed.

> didn't I tuck them in? didn't I tuck the feet away,
> didn't I tuck the sheets in just to keep you out?

cradle, we are cradle, crib, crucible of love.
you cannot tell God from the allowed
shadows.

✧

will.
there is will, lonely and stone in the dark.
that too is gift, raw, like skin, like raft.
who are you to live outside of it?
what made you think you had anything else?
faith like incisors, like hatred is to love.
that too will get you through,
like the thing you thought would get you nowhere.
the thing you thought nothing of, what you thought was
useless, dispensable.
the tiniest thing to love
is everything.

remember, when you wake.

The Angel That Came Through

We do not know his name.
he lurked behind furniture,
took the shape of moths,
took the shape of schedules,
events, and blessed them
behind the ears, with a little
ointment of my blood, and pollen
lost in heaven, when daisies
go to heaven, which they rarely do,
except to earmark my ugly
grief to God's gaze,

and he takes pity.
no, I have earned pity with all my
railing and bombast-heart beating;
I have been loud, deafened monsters
and thin-eared seraphim,
and come home to an empty house,
and found moths.
silent messengering, shuffling dates
and times and hours, so that my bones
could walk through the grating
of air, so hard for me to
delve through by my wits.
so angels passaged me.

the angel that came through.
what is his name?
so anonymous, and unapplauded,
so like my face, to go unnoticed;
so happy among his cohorts, to have been
done with deeds for me,
to have left his slippers around to have me fill them
like a laugh,
that the universe is not so great that
it can't kindness give,

to me, son of horror,
man of ginger envy
and abandonment.

the angel came and clapped my
lungs into awakedom, hope like a stance
where I could lift my head, and smile
resolutely at dawn clouds.

this angel came. in the night, or day,
unruffling the sheets; in the choreography of
garden, he stole into my life, in many
sundry forms, a moth, a waft of wind,
a saddened cloud.

he was not awful with his wings;
like my gossamer, my fear,
he tendered me by what I would not shun –
a friend, a restful breath,
an ideal like a lost heirloom.

and here I am to survive me
in his wake; where no thrashing of air
was, I am a boy again,
born of himself, carried
in the belly of love.

Son

my mother's death.
left me lonely.
as skies and mountains.

there was no call for her to go.
continents and songs mourned her
quietly.

✧

aged crone, stalwart and swan.
how many memories a regalia
in her head?
lyric songs and dead facts.

you are my legs.
whom I look for in the rocks and desert.
stamped with the sunlight, a name
who taught me sun, how it meant
health. I used it at your tombstone while
you slept.

✧

highway, road, films and
laugh and grazing fingers.
pictures of you looking at pictures.

taught things, I am. finishing, an ideal.
your final notes, crowned with a gene
of one of God's perspectives, a way
of saying world freshly.

the enemies of song have come to visit,
mother. rent, disease and folly,
bad dogs.
I try to look at sun and remember faith.
the braille of it, for you, by touch
remembering.

Death Knocks

death knocks, mother of nothing.
I dreamt I ran into aunt margaret;
we were almost happy to see each other,
though she was dead.

I dreamt I was lost in wal-mart.
things are almost the same.

I dreamt God gave me fifty thousand years
to become holy.

I said someday all these young people are
going to be strangers. I shall want love
from strangers, and I'd best prepare
to love.
I'd best not stall on love,
for the way I look up at Him
is the way I look at others,
or the way I will be able to or can.
He will not know me,
for I did not feed, clothe and give drink to etc.

I am the smallest of his little ones too.
I have had my hands out,
all my five thousand mouths,
for years. I have been trying to drink
from the stone wall, the world.

it occurs to me it would not happen, this
contradiction, this needing more than others,
except that I am encased where the heart
cannot fly.
it occurs to me the heart was not meant
for arms and legs, but for seeing through
and having thoughts of the other;
and a lifetime is about teaching the heart to
imagine in one cell.

also the heart is about freedom dragging its
bones like tin cans to a cat's tail,
of how the body can be ignored for
periods of time, or how it can be made
metaphors for heart.
the body is a cousin that comes and goes,
and the heart is a mothering thing
unlike death.

today I will find aunt margaret.
I will not be lost in wal-mart
and I will be at home with
vicious children.
I will do the impossible
and lose my bad dreams,
for no heroic reason,
for everything calls me
to try out
mortality.
and finally, one thing is the same
as another – a clue, a sign,
and a small angel,
to make the moment,
arbitrarily, meaning.
I do not have a lot of time,
and suddenly it seems the fifty thousand years
I have had so many times is nothing but hope,
and suddenly the body stutters,
the heart flies out, becomes bird
and mother, and I am not running too far from
her, as she calls me to myself.

Ramble

look how these bones assuage
nothing, climb nothing, amount to less.
look how the green blossoms are up to
par better than my bones. how I am nothing,
but beauty mustered,
spirited.

look how they make their way up hills,
down hills, this sack of bones,
this concatenation, god-desirer.

bricolage, I could call it, well of artifacts
going back to childhood, ball thrower,
love-destroyer,

these bones that took me up steep canyons,
down love's slender arms,
pillared in fire, for Him,
dead wood, tinder, so much
beachwood, food for his
maw you might say,
lover of earth that earth will take back.

and hurt, much like the heart,
aching, wanting to be spirit.
I shall assuage you, my thin wonders.

we shall be free of the rhetoric of air
and road.
I shall make you a candle, a prayer
of my days, I shall have you walking
to your desired place, I shall make
of you a story.
I shall say, this is what they were meant for,
these bones, ignorant flowery ones,
that did not know, like a dog, where
I was going.

Alive Again

slam, bam,
the boomerang
of pain, the suffering.

the comedian at work again,
almighty God who kills my loved ones
to perfect someone other, something
other,
to straighten us out, to bring us to our knees,
to get us to absolve grass, wind, hair,
to get us reduced to a tiny particle of
heart,
obeisance to stars and moonlight.

I am defeated oh Lord, at once, of my own
will, 'cause like a landlord you have all the time in the
world to evict me or scheme me
an open door. I haven't the wits
to plot my happiness or your design.
I am, hands up, a lunatic bequest; I am shrivelling
host of grace, I am question salivating for
embodied love, I am prayer-maker for
the murdered, murdering.

I am all yours, scared least of all by anything
but my own resistance, that scars me, traps me like
a broken beetle in a country room.
false lights, ceilings... I am trapped in the conundrum,
brain, swatted by my needs, on the rotted planks
of homes I built.

I am beaten thin as sheet metal in the Sparrow's Mills.
I am wispier than my most delicate thirteen year
old thoughts, so far away by now.

I am had, and wonderfully dead
to plan either my horror or my
smile,
Saviour; I move through the motions of my sin
and charity like magicians' hands minus the rabbits
and doves.

Almighty comedic one whose comedy
is my abasement into a flower
I cannot understand, whose beauty of me is
beyond and so abhorrent...
that I cannot smile is my ticket to your heart,
that I cannot mourn is the sign of my loving...
that I have no anger, hunger or response,
is the beginning,
a prayer, as I was in the beginning,
denuded, hankering for the first ray of light,
any blessed thing I learned to call my own,
stupidly.

It is care for the beetle I have, wondering at last
if it will die or find release; and if I open the door
for it, am I like much of the world? – the
inadvertent, slight touch of mercy, like anything upon
me, like this world, of you.

Confession

only beauty you refresh me
sinful man

I have failed the bushes, lilacs,
pretty things
I have failed firelight

I have not let birds in,
nor fed the animals
I have hurt clouds
and cursed leaves

I have let music be unheard
and not watched steam rise from
the kettle

I have let photographs gather dust
and not rejoiced in the smile of
a certain year.
I have given away what I did not have
and taken what I could not use

and I have looked up to you oh God
and wasted breath

time too I have let fall
from the eaves and icicles
and not taken refuge in the
leaves that were an alcove
to my boyhood

I have loved glass
and shiny bits of houses not my own
and given words that became lonely
as they wandered

I have failed my love
for squandering my abundance,
the surplus of creation

I have come to others
all these things
aborted in me
and found metaphors
to take their place

I have also killed myself
for love of the man
who loved the things I love,

my brother and my child;
because I did not love him simply
I gave him food he could not eat

and now he walks in the other room
still alive
and I am not joined to him

who needed nothing.

How to Give in the World

there is a laugh that makes me cry
when I hear it in my heart...
let it be taken from me.

for it clots the stars and sundry gifts.
it's the laugh I lived for, the kind you work
your life to hear again,
the laugh of the beloved,
the kind that trumpets
blue-bells, buttercups,
for a man who could see them,
if grace walked down the street.

there is this laugh that you should take from me,
and the memory of grace. take that too.
for it leaks from me
and disposes me to
nothing.

it was my purpose –
to give to someone in just such a way
as to bring laughter to their eyes.
I have these hands and
a walk that goes around the planet in a flash
and I am paralyzed from birds
and evening sun.

I wait for the right key to one of many houses where,
trapped, is the laugh I must set free.

but it is colours I must learn.
the colour of a closed door,
an open one. I must learn to read
complexions, the right day, the right hour.

teach me snow and wind,
and how these things fulfill the world
without me.

and let me not be there when my love sings.

Changed

the night I became a priest
it rained, dully, washing me,
and didn't wash away the masterpiece,
the colours didn't run, not red, like blood;
the night I became a priest I merely
wept and prayed devoutly
that someone's life might be spared
for my own; the night
my soul came back,
I loved someone better than myself,
with no more dread
of murdering.

let's say there were four angels
that accompanied me and brought
meaning, hope and peace, and the fourth
brought back something that escapes me now,
because it redeems me.

hungry fella that I am,
and I do not even know it, calling myself cool
when hot, and dull when awake, and caring
when dead.
I know nothing of my desire,
until the night I became a priest
and wanted to let everything live.

it doesn't seem so bad, the rain on me,
dull, in the woods; as if I had no skin,
I remember the boy I was, how he would have
hated being so naked under God and stars;
and here I am almost transmogrified,
blowing a kiss to the boy I was,
half fathering him, and looking up,
am fathered.

Transmogrified

and these the bees and flowers
are yours too.
and my hips and assorted brain-
griefs, and airways for planes
and clouds, a dead girl's heart,
my mother's escape through to
arcturus or one or other galaxy
through her tombstone.
            much.
and hope, you send.
leaves and their amazing chlorophyll
though I don't think they have so much
as the radiant sides of your smile
when you are not bleating will
and dire behest.

I'd like to walk into the next day of my life,
not so much without you
as with myself and the illusion of doing it all,
neatly, which perhaps is what it is, our will
not so different from the utter everything
that's ours when we arraign our joy onto
your means; free will only in your grace,
they say,
and dandelions too, they turn from yellow
to white. would that I could, so gingerly,
without bleeding the planks of my brain.
and so, black-eyed susans I spotted today, they are
the beginning of several thousand other
things I almost saw but could not, dropped into
the pit of shilly-shally, hurt and scar.
one day I will see it all, said like a visitor
to a new land, like a lousy tourist
presupposing, what? – the gift of life?

ah look how you take a break today
from tasking me, and running my will through
the stem of my brain like forced shoots.
today is respite. airplanes mosey across the sky,
birds congregate on this tree and that, and
I can tell, no one is dying whom I know so well.
I would feel it, if they were, like your breath on me
this moment, for which my skin is goosy for the
vellum of hope you thread to the underside of it
like some skilled surgeon.

very well, I take you, gracefully, and let my
ventricles on one side be wafted
by your grace, while the deadened parts
wait to resuscitate like the yellow to puffs
of dandelions. so much analogy, don't you
think? – to wink at you, through cloud
and cloud-cover, my sun for whom I bask
like a mermaid holding a man's beating heart,
weening your ocean, which I must be,
your element, not transmogrified as yet –
man, not yet your arms,
not yet relaxed into the brash melody
of hope and death.

Desert Song 2

sometimes you are just grateful
if anyone comes through the door.

sometimes you think you have hurt
everyone and everyone has hurt you,
and will,
sometimes the time of divinizing birds
arrives, of figuring out their westerly
movements, or why they try to fly
through your window with a thud
after a long winter.
like us they are dazed and seek for shelter
in anything, even the house of a confused man.

sometimes you create because it is
just the thing to do, and what you create is
inadvertent, like a house for birds,
or like guests who come not knowing they
bail a man out of loneliness; sometimes a poem
will come that has no joy and it will go to someone
like a divinizing.

even a death has use, or anything you do
that is your ignorance.
what you brought was not what was needed.
what you did not know you had was plenty,
like pockets for the wind.
you provide, dutifully, the body of God,
running his fingers down the strands of creation,
and it seems like meagre employment
to the imagined stars that nurse you, like
a houselight as you stumble home.

sometimes you wish anyone would come
and fill the voice of sunlight.
but someday I will spell things as they are...
the dawn, the branch, the moment,
they will come to me sufficient, and I shall
feel like a man and I will go out and second
guess nothing among the people and leaves,
lonely for nothing. that too shall be my dream
and the birds will fly westerly and I will not wonder
at a home for them or what I can provide.

and most importantly I will paint myself into
my life and not stop there.
I may inhabit myself, and lovely sets of eyes will
look in and see as plain a thing
as me,
like a repository, like a reservoir for the
uninspired... that which around me hungers at this
very moment like desire.

someday desire will look like what it is.
the fulfilled, looking back on itself.
and I shall feel useful, like a loving thing,
not dazzled by will or cheap magic,
much less by my commotion, but
by His servitude.

God as Moths

1

I will not kill this one.
he is large and hides
and comes out of shadows,
big as a pet;
he is neither worm nor butterfly,
he is a mystery thing looking for light,
like me.
he is my brother,
I will let in and out.
I hurt him inadvertently,
and he springs back to life.

2

this one clung to the night window,
spread like a cross,
a cross resting.

he brought a tiny saviour through the dark.
he is a breath against my face.
he waits.
the kitchen light; false light, or daylight,
it does not matter, he is not fussy.
I should be happy in my ignorant life.

3

the smaller ones flit in and out.
I no sooner open the door than they follow
me in, companions, careful doves,
lost souls of those who loved me.
they wait at the houselight for me,
to see what I have been up to.
hushed, so hushed.
like the mute hand of Him
on my shoulder.

4

now He is telling me
by His wing on sin
and wayward,
so gentle, this awesome
perpetrator of sea and pole,
He deigns a little finger
on the obtrusive dark,
like a child carried across
the battlefield,
He sends a motherly feather,
He sends a sliver of my conscience.
He is in the room with me.
the mighty into the hapless,
in no found thing,
but moth.

5

one day I put my face to
the bark of a tree, and heard
my blood shoots, heard earth stirring
in its taps, the water that must come
when I am drained of love.
pale and drawn from the surface planet,
tired as the old tree, I kissed my brethren,
the beaten, weathered, who had been standing in
the cold all winter long,
and I heard the tap roots, a gurgle,
something saved, like spring.

moth too, is saved of me.
the silence of my soul,
spared of me,
like memory
of the good I am.

6

and now one comes,
a sheen on its wings. this one different from
all the others; a silver sheen,
that is not like a crown
nor the hope I make of dumb things,
but like
leaves in the rush of wind,
what tracks me to Him.

so many angel messengers.
all with his kiss on my nape.
so many eyes on Him,
all with my desire.

Surrounding Angels

so tired
and ready for heaven
as the moth lands on the fridge
door
so tired, for a bit of charity from
the open hand, so eager
for the faces of my loved ones; so tired of
running everywhere but to Him,
my fabric, who has walked in me,
whom I have walked through to
be myself.

so ready for the bed,
and the unreproaching song of skylarks,
the home and the bridge,
the river, the dream;

so tired of waking to a full-fledged sky
not yet of Him.

que sera, sera and the
meaning twirls; even for this, even for
doris day singing I am nostalgic.
all loved things are my gentle animals,

as the moth follows me, I pray it lands on
my shoulder, as God enters the room, I pray
that I spread my arms that are not wings,
and include myself in the embrace of Him.
for I have so much pity for a boy so tired
from walking on a man's legs, with a man's thoughts,
so tired and ready for heaven
like a thing to lay his head on.

as the moth lands on the fridge, I am so gentle
with lame things and small.
it is my tiredness makes me gentle, I know that.
perhaps one day I will be light as air, wispy as
light, and I will fill things, become things and
be embodied, and I shall change
into courageous love.

At the Colorado

Nobody cares.
Let them not fool you with
Their obvious needs and obtuse
Cries.

You are left alone in the dark with a
Clutched rosary and the tear of
Yesterday like a snow globe. You turn it
Over, around and around. It is the same face
Staring at you, the little boy you loved, the evil man
You became... they are all lovable and ready for
Forgiveness.

It does not matter what car you get into, which
Apple tree you climb. It is the same view, the valley
You would have lain down in, asleep, or happy or joyful.
That you didn't have company doesn't seem surprising.

But you would travel now to other valleys
And the time is short.

Wake me Father, from the dream of myself.
Let me walk in the dream of another that I may
Bless what I could not find sacred of myself.
I have learned so much about blessing from the almanac of
Laugh and kiss – I am ready to hold butterflies and watch
Them be birds, or simple trajectories like boys becoming
What they wanted. I am ready to be and let be,

In a world that cares less and so is ready to have your
Entry like a mediator
With his hair on fire for all the auburn myths, remembered nights
All come to visit like a bestowal.

I am ready to redeem the world with what I have lost.
So giving an immolation I would not have wanted, but a gift

Of the discarded, forever useful by His will.
However unwanting the world is, let me offer it my hands,
To drink from the imagined, when it will need imagining.
In return I ask nothing, but to be like a river,
And to join hands with the sea, or to be lost simply
Among the stones and brush of an undivided land,
Spent on Your providence, while the bright fish leap
For joy in the forgetting sun.

Supplanting

look, exchanged for,
blood and muse. dead, for life,
love for fathering.

look, so much exchanged for –
hanging face for spirit,
sex for animus,
dawn for heartache.

exchanged so much for
Him, cool afficionado,
limb-taker, cup-savager,
my very own dandy locks
for leave-taking. anointer.
fear Him.
He knows and loves you
cooingly, rips open stars and
entrails,
like a music. you will not hear
this making
of you. you will not hear
the soul branded,
what flower you
will be, awakened.

Easter

how many deaths are there
how many deaths can there be
I have tasted a blue one, green one, the kind that
came with kisses and brightness, the kind that came
with the tremor of bone;
the kind that came with kindness,
the most cruel – the death of that which was
distilled by simple want,
and hope.
the death of hope, that was the best,
the one that left us foetus-like in Your palm;
the death of hope was hardest,
it left us wondering why You left it lying around
after new beginnings and burials.
there wasn't an easier way to kill the skin?
what is it in the human that is renegade from You,
with every trust and beauty that does not remark
on You?
very well.
I have no hope today in the substantial.
I will admit that one more cup of coffee is hope
enough, and when I cannot raise my hand
I will waft my heart up from my mouth
by simple wishing, and when that is taken too,
I will be still as moss and leaf, and be filled
with sun, and I will say that it is You,
as I do now.

be sun to me, for I can no more till my garden
than I can arrange for myself a plan
of caring.
the orchestra of spring is what I most
bow to, respectful of leaf and badger,

and wait for Your presiding touch,
and I must ignore the corpses behind the hedge
and fence, the beauties and the loved,
and smell like resurrection.
and kiss You like a face upturned to cloud
and weather, a simple man made coward
and made clean.

The Prayer

Here are two stars, in different colours.
Here are the northern lights, opening and
shutting their lattices. Here is warm snow,
and stones in the wavelets,
trees lit and unlit.
My hands unlatch the night.
I walk through to the altar,
the madonna on my right,
in the chapel breath.

It is my breath, the stars an exhalation.

Acknowledgements

As always my heartfelt thanks to Dennis Lee for his comprehending judgement and inspiration. Belated and sincere thanks to Albert Moritz for his editorial input and longstanding friendship. To Rishma Dunlop for her artistic acumen and boundless generosity. To Fr. Robert Nusca and Monsignor John Murphy for their presbyteral support. To Bill and Jean Gairdner for their roast lamb and sane grasp of the world. To Susan Perly for conversations that brought eloquence to my wilderness. To Isabella Colallilo Katz for her empathic gifts. To Damiano Pietropaolo for refurbishing rooms in the house of dreams. To Glen McGuire, for his untiring faith. To Andy Vergalito and Joey Delamarina for the Niagara Falls I return to when my spirit wearies. And to Ian Lancashire for reminding me of an ethic we grow nostalgic of.

Pier Giorgio Di Cicco
was born in Arezzo, Italy, and raised in
Montreal, Toronto and Baltimore.
He currently lives in Toronto.